AF270486

NORSE MYTHOLOGY

FENRIR

BY AMY C. REA

Kids Core

An Imprint of Abdo Publishing
abdobooks.com

abdobooks.com

Published by Abdo Publishing, a division of ABDO, PO Box 398166, Minneapolis, Minnesota 55439. Copyright © 2024 by Abdo Consulting Group, Inc. International copyrights reserved in all countries. No part of this book may be reproduced in any form without written permission from the publisher. Kids Core™ is a trademark and logo of Abdo Publishing.

Printed in the United States of America, North Mankato, Minnesota.
052023
092023

THIS BOOK CONTAINS
RECYCLED MATERIALS

Cover Photos: Shutterstock Images, (Fenrir, background)
Interior Photos: Shutterstock Images, 4–5, 9, 10, 17 (paw print), 17 (beard), 17 (ribbon), 28 (top), 29 (bottom); Science History Images/Alamy, 7, 29 (top); Martin Oldenbourg/Walhall, die Götterwelt der Germanen, 12–13, 28 (bottom); Charles Walker Collection/Alamy, 15; Art Malivanov/Shutterstock Images, 17 (cat); Good Studio/Shutterstock Images, 17 (bear, bird); Mironova Iuliia/Shutterstock Images, 17 (fish); Mary Desy/Shutterstock Images, 17 (mountain); Roland Topor/Shutterstock Images, 17 (roots); ART Collection/Alamy, 18; H.A. Guerber/Myths of the Norsemen from the Eddas and Sagas, 20; Martin Mecnarowski/Shutterstock Images, 22–23; Werner Forman/Universal Images Group/Getty Images, 25; James Thompson/Stockimo/Alamy, 26

Editor: Katharine Hale
Series Designer: Katharine Hale

Library of Congress Control Number: 2022949118

Publisher's Cataloging-in-Publication Data

Names: Rea, Amy C., author.
Title: Fenrir / by Amy C. Rea
Description: Minneapolis, Minnesota: Abdo Publishing Company, 2024 | Series: Norse mythology | Includes online resources and index.
Identifiers: ISBN 9781098291174 (lib. bdg.) | ISBN 9781098277352 (ebook)
Subjects: LCSH: Mythology, Norse--Juvenile literature. | Wolves--Juvenile literature. | Animals, Mythical--Juvenile literature. | Fictitious animals-- Juvenile literature.
Classification: DDC 293.13--dc23

CONTENTS

Fenrir is a giant wolf from
Norse mythology.

CHAPTER 1

THE CHAINING OF FENRIR

Fenrir was a wolf. He was raised by Odin and the other gods. The god Tyr was the only one brave enough to feed him. Fenrir grew and grew. Soon, he was giant. The gods were all scared of him. They decided something must be done.

The gods challenged Fenrir. They would chain him up. Then he would see if he was strong enough to break the chains. Fenrir broke them easily. This was a fun game! The gods did this twice. Then they challenged Fenrir a third time. This time, the chain looked like a ribbon. Fenrir was suspicious. He thought the chain might be magic. Fenrir would only allow himself to be tied up if one of the gods put his hand in Fenrir's mouth. Tyr bravely volunteered. He put his hand in Fenrir's mouth while the gods wrapped the chain around the wolf.

Fenrir had been right. This chain was magic, and it was unbreakable. Fenrir was trapped! He was furious. He howled and raged, biting off Tyr's hand as revenge.

Tyr sacrificed his hand so the gods could chain Fenrir.

Norse Mythology

Fenrir's story is part of Norse mythology. Most surviving Norse myths come from **Scandinavia**. They are written in the Old Norse language. These stories tell the religious beliefs of early northern Germanic peoples. Norse mythology

Norse Werewolves

Wolves appear in many Norse myths. In one myth, two thieves came to a wealthy person's home. They stole wolfskins and put them on. But the skins made the thieves turn into wolves. They attacked other humans and even each other. Eleven days later, they turned back into humans. They burned the wolfskins so no one else would suffer the same way.

Frost giants appear in many Norse myths.

explained their world's history and future. The stories have gods and goddesses, giants, elves, and magical dwarfs.

Norse mythology says Fenrir will kill Odin at Ragnarok.

Fenrir was an important part of Norse mythology. A **prophecy** said Fenrir and his siblings would harm the gods. The Norse people believed an event called Ragnarok would destroy the world and the gods. Then the world would start again. Stories said Fenrir and his siblings would be part of Ragnarok. Fenrir would break out of his chains and swallow Odin.

Joshua J. Mark writes about ancient history. In an article about Fenrir, he wrote:

> Although Fenrir is understood as . . . one of the "villains" of the story of Ragnarok, the original story makes clear that Odin's and the other gods' treatment of the great wolf contributed to his siding with the forces of chaos against them.

Source: Joshua J. Mark. "Fenrir." *World History Encyclopedia*, 25 Aug. 2021, www.worldhistory.org. Accessed 22 Sept. 2022.

Point of View

What is the author's point of view on this topic? What is your point of view? Write a short essay about how they are similar and different.

Jormungandr, Hel, and Fenrir are Loki's children with the giantess Angrboda.

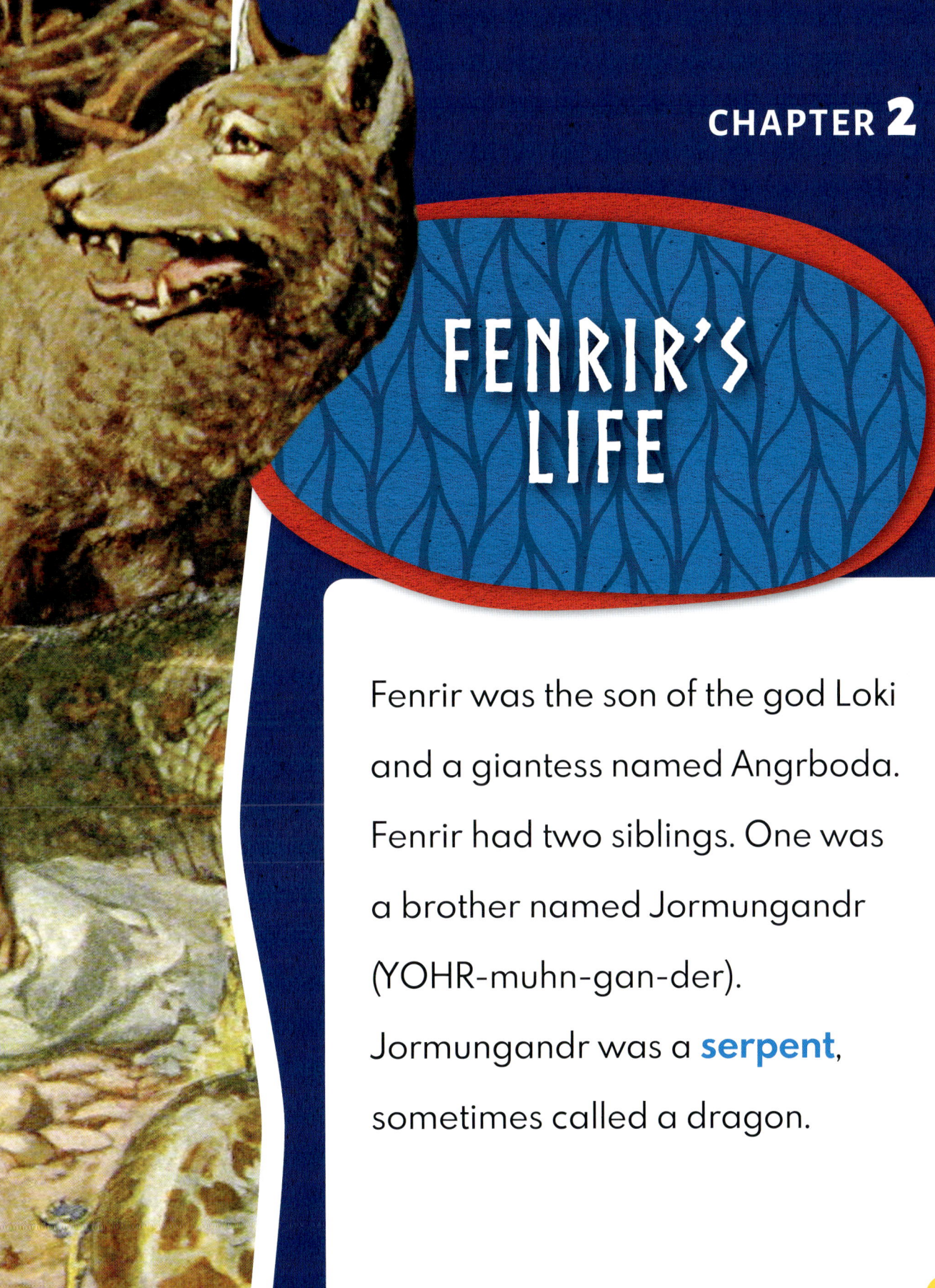

CHAPTER 2

FENRIR'S LIFE

Fenrir was the son of the god Loki and a giantess named Angrboda. Fenrir had two siblings. One was a brother named Jormungandr (YOHR-muhn-gan-der). Jormungandr was a **serpent**, sometimes called a dragon.

Fenrir's sister Hel was half woman and half **corpse**. The three siblings lived with their mother in Jotunheim, the land of the giants.

One day, Odin received a prophecy. It told him that Loki's children would destroy the gods. Odin wanted to destroy them before they could destroy him. But when he met Fenrir, Odin decided not to kill him. Instead, the gods raised him. They hoped they could prevent

The Fate of Fenrir's Siblings

Fenrir's brother Jormungandr and sister Hel were part of the prophecy that said they would destroy the gods. Odin hurled Jormungandr into the sea. He dropped Hel into Niflheim, the Norse land of the dead.

Norse mythology says Fenrir and Jormungandr will battle the gods at Ragnarok.

the prophecy. But Fenrir grew to be so big that the gods became afraid of him. They could not control him.

Making Gleipnir

Odin and other gods made a strong chain called Loeding. But Fenrir easily broke it. The gods built a stronger chain called Dromi. But Fenrir broke that chain just as easily.

Odin remembered that there were dwarfs in the world below him. They were excellent chain-makers. Odin sent a messenger to them. He asked them to make a chain Fenrir could not break.

The dwarfs sent the gods a chain called Gleipnir. This chain was made of things that were hard to find. Odin asked Fenrir to try his strength for the third time.

Trapped!

What looked like a weak ribbon was a strong chain. The harder Fenrir fought, the tighter it held him. Fenrir bit off Tyr's hand, howling with rage. The gods were excited. They had finally trapped Fenrir! But he was still dangerous.

Building an Unbreakable Chain

The footsteps
of a cat

The beard
of a woman

The roots of
a mountain

The breath
of a fish

The sinews
of a bear
(sinews connect
muscle to bone and
are very strong)

Hair ribbon

The saliva
of a bird

The dwarfs had special ways of finding things that others could not find. A cat's footsteps are almost silent. Fish do not breathe air. But somehow the dwarfs found all these things. They used them to make Gleipnir.

According to one myth, Fenrir drooled when his jaws were forced open. His saliva formed the river Ván.

The gods forced a large sword between Fenrir's jaws. Fenrir could no longer bite or howl. Then the gods chained him to a stone on an island.

Fenrir would remain chained until he was released on the day of Ragnarok.

Fenrir's Children

Some stories say Fenrir had two children with a giantess. Their names were Skoll and Hati. These wolves would also play a role in Ragnarok.

In Norse mythology, the sun and moon are pulled through the sky by **chariots**. Sol, whose name means sun, drives the sun's chariot. Her brother Mani, whose name means moon, drives the moon's chariot. Skoll and Hati chase after the sun and moon. It is not clear from the myths which wolf chases the sun and which chases the moon. Different stories say different things.

Some scholars think stories about Skoll and Hati may have originally been about Fenrir. Over time, storytellers added different wolves to the stories.

Eventually, Skoll and Hati will catch and eat the sun and moon. This will send the world into darkness. Then all chains will break, and Fenrir will be freed. Ragnarok will begin.

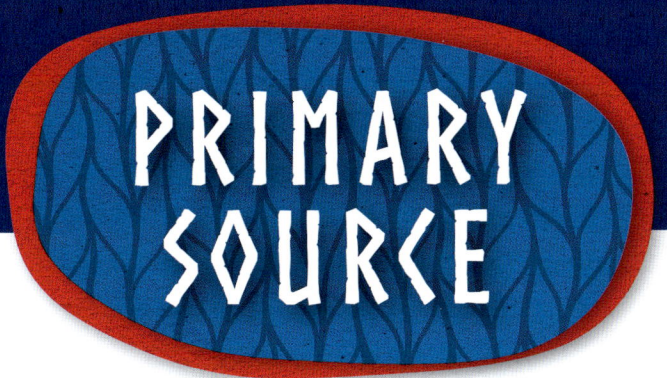
In the poem *Lokasenna*, or "Loki's Taunts," Loki taunts Tyr for losing his hand to Fenrir. Tyr responds:

> I lost that hand,
>
> you lost that son;
>
> we both suffered loss.
>
> Your son isn't doing well, either;
>
> he remains forever in chains,
>
> waiting for Ragnarok.

Source: Jackson Crawford, translator. *The Poetic Edda: Stories of the Norse Gods and Heroes.* Hackett, 2015, p. 108.

What's the Big Idea?

What is this quote's main idea? Explain how the main idea is supported by details.

Wolves once roamed most of the Northern Hemisphere. Their populations are much smaller today.

CHAPTER 3

FENRIR'S INFLUENCE

Wolves hunt their **prey** in groups called packs. The Norse people also needed to hunt for food. They used animal skins to make blankets and clothes. Wolves were **competition**. They were dangerous. But the Norse people did not only fear wolves.

They respected wolves for their strength and ability to hunt.

People could not control wolves. The same is true for Fenrir. Even though the gods manage to chain him up, they cannot keep him chained forever. Fenrir would break free at Ragnarok.

Fenrir in Books

Fenrir has inspired modern writers. There is a wolf called Fenris Wolf in the Magnus Chase and the Gods of Asgard series by Rick Riordan. A werewolf called Fenrir Greyback is a villain in J. K. Rowling's Harry Potter books. C. S. Lewis named a wolf character Fenris Ulf in the first American edition of *The Lion, the Witch, and the Wardrobe*. In the British edition and later American editions, the wolf is called Maugrim.

The Isle of Man is an island near the United Kingdom. A piece from a Viking cross found there shows Fenrir swallowing Odin at Ragnarok.

A rune stone in Tullstorp, Sweden, shows a wolf and a ship.

He would swallow Odin. The myth shows how powerful the Norse people believed wolves to be.

Not all wolves in Norse mythology are villains. Odin has two pet wolves, Geri and Freki. He feeds them from his table.

Wolves in Art

Fenrir is often seen as powerful and dangerous in art. Some surviving Norse **rune stones** show scenes of Ragnarok. Fenrir is often shown battling Odin. A Norse cross in England shows Odin's son Vidarr killing Fenrir in revenge. Scholars think other surviving Norse art may show Tyr and Fenrir.

Wolves were important to the Norse people and in their mythology. Fenrir is one of the best-known wolves in the myths. According to the Norse people, his power and rage will lead him to help destroy the gods at Ragnarok.

Further Evidence

Visit the website below. Does it give any new evidence to support Chapter Three?

Gray Wolf

abdocorelibrary.com/Fenrir

LEGENDARY FACTS

Norse mythology says Fenrir was a strong, large wolf.

Odin received a prophecy saying that Fenrir and his siblings would destroy the gods. He decided to try to prevent that from happening.

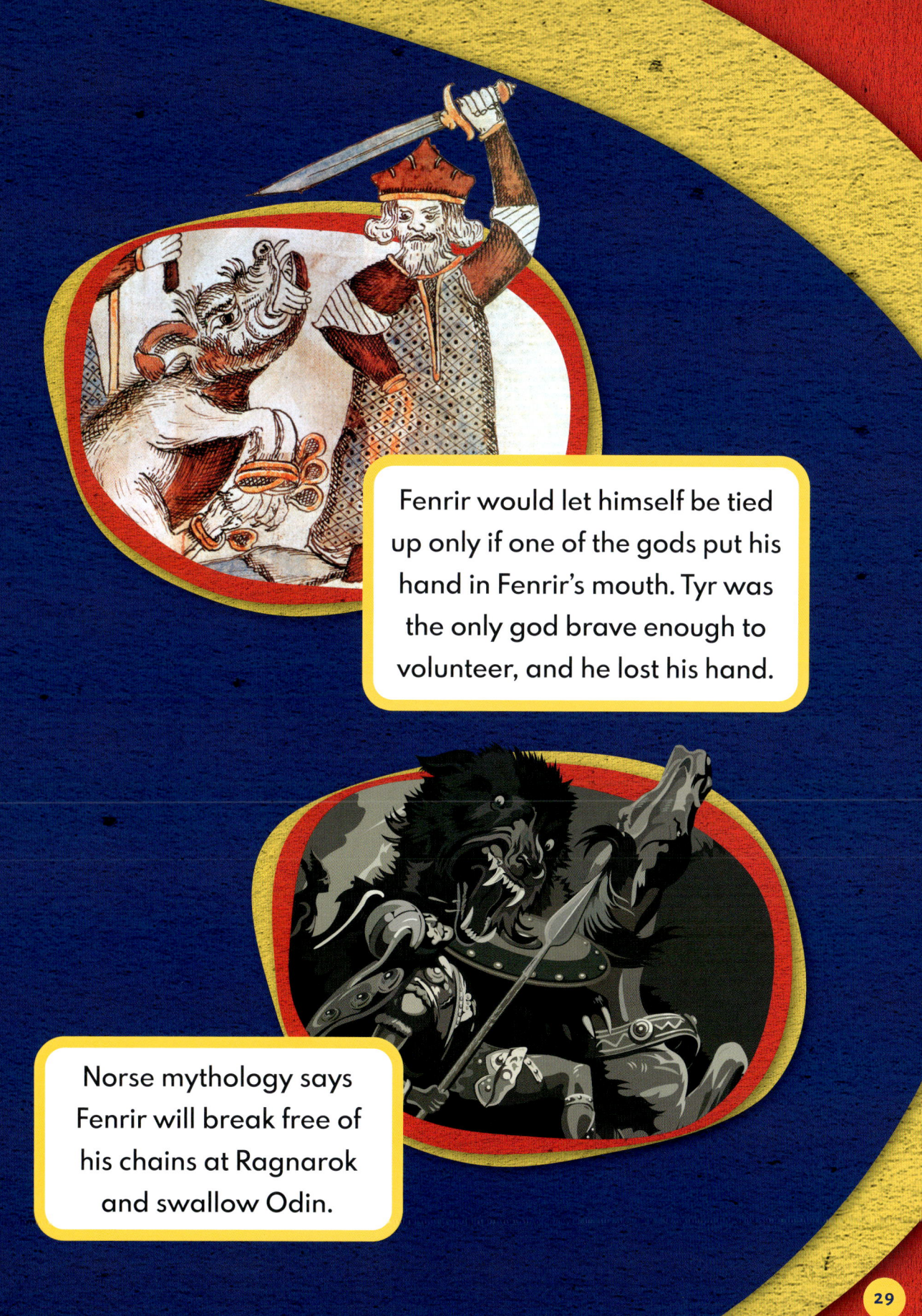

Fenrir would let himself be tied up only if one of the gods put his hand in Fenrir's mouth. Tyr was the only god brave enough to volunteer, and he lost his hand.

Norse mythology says Fenrir will break free of his chains at Ragnarok and swallow Odin.

Glossary

chariot
a small, two-wheeled vehicle that was pulled by animals and was often used for warfare or races

competition
living things fighting over the same resources

corpse
a dead body

prey
an animal that is hunted by other animals

prophecy
a prediction of something that will happen in the future

rune stones
stones carved by Vikings to honor the dead

Scandinavia
the countries of Norway, Sweden, and Denmark, and sometimes Iceland and Finland

serpent
a snake

Online Resources

To learn more about Fenrir, visit our free resource websites below.

Visit **abdocorelibrary.com** or scan this QR code for free Common Core resources for teachers and students, including vetted activities, multimedia, and booklinks, for deeper subject comprehension.

Visit **abdobooklinks.com** or scan this QR code for free additional online weblinks for further learning. These links are routinely monitored and updated to provide the most current information available.

Learn More

Alexander, Heather. *A Child's Introduction to Norse Mythology*. Black Dog & Leventhal, 2018.

Conley, Kate. *Loki*. Abdo, 2024.

Ralphs, Matt. *Norse Myths*. DK Children, 2021.

Index

About the Author

Amy C. Rea is the author of several children's books. She also writes about travel and food in Minnesota. She lives in Saint Anthony, Minnesota, with her husband and silly dog.